MW00960876

Neurodivergent Millionaire

Rebelling Against the Status Quo

Shalese Nicole Heard

Copyright © 2024 Neurodivergent Millionaire

All rights reserved, including the right of reproduction in whole or part in any format. For information regarding bulk purchases of this book, digital purchase, and special discounts, please contact the author.

Table of Contents

CHAPTER 1

What IS Financial Freedom?

Financial Freedom

Financial Empowerment

Financial Independence

They're all the same in a nutshell.

We've all seen the images on social media of yachts, cars, houses, traveling the world, wearing designer labels, and making millions of dollars while you sleep.

While these things CAN be part of financial empowerment, freedom, and independence; there is a bigger picture here:

Being independent of ableist systems, toxic relationships, and situations where you aren't your best self.

Financial freedom, empowerment and independence involves living in a state of peace, where you aren't worried about meeting your obligations all while you are able to engage in your passions, special interests, and work that plays up your strengths.

Financial freedom, empowerment and independence doesn't involve you overexerting yourself to work on your "weaknesses" just to endure a bad fitting job to pay the bills. It involves you doing work you love, that comes easy to you and focuses on your strengths. THAT is how you create easy money without living in lack.

Here are some scenarios to drive the point home:

You've got a millionaire with 3 yachts, a mansion, a Maserati, and all the luxury designer labels. He works a job he hates, a job that stresses him out and brings out his weaknesses. He is surrounded by toxic people day in and day out. He doesn't get any time to care for himself. His relationships and health suffer. He cannot be true to himself; he is constantly walking on eggshells to maintain what he has. Everything he does is centered around making ends meet, to keep up that lifestyle.

In this situation, the millionaire is NOT financially free, empowered, or independent.

His things and money control HIM instead of HIM controlling his things and his money.

On the other hand, you've got a college student. She studies what she is passionate about, can afford her passion for art and music. She chooses to forgo owning a vehicle and chooses to live in a studio apartment. She has the freedom to work with only the people she feels comfortable with and can carefully choose her environment. She has time to do all the things that are important to her, all while having the finances to fund what is important to her.

This college student has more financial freedom, empowerment, and independence despite not having the material wealth that the billionaire has. She gets to lead a less stressful life, where she can be true to herself and still create a life around everything that is important to her.

Ultimately, being a Neurodivergent Millionaire is all about creating a life around what is important to YOU. Whether it's a mansion and 3 yachts, or your best RV Life!

CHAPTER 2

Myths about how to achieve Financial Freedom

We've been fed plenty of lies about money and what it takes to achieve financial freedom. Let's dispel them:

Getting a college degree guarantees job security.

We have all been told this lie throughout our childhood. Go to school, take out tons of student loans, and major in anything because going to school to get that degree is always worth it. Many of us fell for it, especially those of us in the Neurodivergent community who were taught to believe that formal education would increase our options and make it easier to find work. In many cases, you are possibly better off starting a business, or learning a trade.

What these colleges DON'T tell us is that it is much harder for us on average to secure gainful employment, because of ableist hiring practices and lack of appropriate accommodations at work.

We often graduate school only to find ourselves struggling to even get the most basic, entry level position due to lack of understanding and accommodation from employers.

Even if we do secure the job, the job may prove to create burnout for us quickly, or the work environment can prove too toxic, or we find that the work doesn't play up our strengths well.

Formal education isn't always the best way for us as Neurodivergent folk to build financial freedom. It often hinders us more than it helps us in the long run.

If you have something specific you want to do, or if you find it fulfilling to obtain higher education, do so. Just don't do it believing it's the only path to financial security. Check your mindset and the myths you were told before pursuing higher education.

Working a 9-5 is the only way to build financial independence.

Working a 9-5 isn't always lucrative enough to build a quality of life. Depending on the job, you might find yourself unfulfilled, stressed out constantly and not even earning enough to create a meaningful savings account, or save for future purchases. This is one of the biggest myths out there.

Working hard at a job is always better than being on any benefit program.

This isn't always the case. Let's consider this scenario:

Someone is receiving $741 for SSI benefits, Medicare, getting their student loans discharged, housing assistance, food assistance, (and depending on your state, other supplemental assistance).

Said person receiving the SSI benefits could only manage to find a part time job paying $500 a month prior to getting SSI. With this job, they get NO benefits, no assistance with housing, no student loan discharge, no healthcare, and limited food benefits.

In this case, working isn't worth it compared to receiving benefits.

In another scenario: you've got a gainfully employed professional who obtained a Graduate degree. They obtain a position in their field that promises stability, great benefits, and growth. However, the cost of living in the area is exorbitant. The salary is still not enough to afford a basic apartment, to pay for their healthcare and retirement benefits, etc.... In fact, their salary is barely covering the basics. They live paycheck to paycheck still. They make JUST ABOVE the threshold to qualify for housing, food, or healthcare programs. At a salary JUST ABOVE the threshold, they are still responsible for paying their student loans.

This is yet another situation where working isn't always worth it. What is even more mind-blowing about this scenario is that it involves doing all the "right things" our elders, parents, teachers told us to do: go to school, get that education, secure that good job. You do all of that, and it STILL doesn't guarantee a comfortable living. This further proves my

point earlier about why the College Degree-Good Job dream Millennials and Gen Z generations were sold on isn't all we were promised it was.

Paying creditors is more important than pursuing the things that bring you joy.

We all need small pleasures in life to keep us encouraged, and to make us feel worthy. Paying a creditor, especially if it's an old bill that has no immediate benefit for paying them, is just a waste of money many times. Paying old debts doesn't increase your credit score significantly. You may as well spend that money on something that brings you joy and makes life feel worth living. Let me be clear here: I'm not saying to be reckless, overspend and not care about keeping your bills current. If it is within your means and ability; always pay your creditors. If you don't have to use credit, don't. Avoid unnecessary debt as much as possible. I am making this point because a lot of people fall into hard times, they have exorbitant medical expenses, or simply don't earn enough to avoid using their credit cards. If you are doing your best and STILL end up in the red, then I see no point in punishing yourself even further by throwing money down the drain.

Anyone who doesn't buy into the American dream is lazy.

The definition of the American Dream is based on consumerism, the status quo and capitalism. There are many people who find fulfillment in other ways besides the standardized American Dream. Furthermore, the American Dream is inaccessible to many marginalized people, due to a laundry list of systemic barriers. Not chasing the American Dream doesn't make a person lazy.

Social media ruins your career.

Social media can HELP your career prospects if you use it to educate and create value for an audience. Increasing numbers of employers are beginning to embrace candidates who use social media for a positive purpose. Additionally, social media can open a variety of business opportunities for you. Having social media profiles, and a niche can help you build an audience to sell digital products to, be considered for

speaking engagements, and even brand deals. Social media oftentimes can be more lucrative than your traditional jobs.

The only way to build wealth is to deny small pleasures and deprive yourself because it's "disciplined".

Depriving yourself has the opposite effect. It makes you feel so discouraged in your savings goals, or earnings goals that you give up and give into overspending. Depriving yourself causes you to develop a mindset of: "I'll never make it, so I may as well just spend everything I have". This is a dangerous mindset to have and can make your financial situation worse by creating a sense of hopelessness. That is the opposite of empowering. Treat Yourself!

CHAPTER 3

Cost of being Neurodivergent.

Being Neurodivergent in this society is expensive as ever. Most people don't realize just how costly it is existing in such an ableist society. The following is a list of common expenses associated with being neurodivergent.

Loss of job opportunities due to employer discrimination.

It is against the law to discriminate against an employee who has a disability. However, employers find ways around that. The hiring process, and interviewing process is inherently ableist. The interview process is abstract, and relies on social cues, following social norms and "reading between the lines". In addition to that, employers are reluctant to hire someone with a disability because they see them as a liability rather than a potential asset. This comes from the negative stigma surrounding having a disability. This is a big reason why we have 85% of Autistic adults either unemployed or underemployed. It's hindering our financial growth.

Having to take time off due to the extra stress that excessive demands create.

Many jobs aren't Neurodivergent friendly, and place undue stress on neurodivergent employees. Unrealistic expectations, a fast-paced environment and difficulty with relating to the social landscape in the workplace leads to neurodivergent employees taking time off to regroup. Paid time off, and paid vacations aren't always an option either, which is a hinderance to earning potential.

Dependence on toxic relationships for financial support, where these people hinder your progress.

Many neurodivergent folks are forced to rely on family, or romantic partners for financial support. This often creates a toxic, disempowering dynamic where the person offering the support feels entitled to mistreat the person whom they are supporting, degrading them, and killing their confidence to purse business or career opportunities that can be life changing.

Medical costs.

In general, people with disabilities on average incur more medical costs, and insurance companies are often reluctant to cover the costs if they are extensive and depending on the nature of incidents. This gets super expensive.

Extra costs for housing (such as needing to live on your own because having a roommate is unbearable).

As Neurodivergent folk, keeping up with us daily is stressful enough. It is stressful enough making sure to meet our obligations, hold a job, build a business, attend to relationships, and practice self-care; having a roommate creates unpredictability and extra stress that can go over the edge. It's often easier for many of us to manage living alone, which is exorbitantly expensive.

CHAPTER 4

How do we rebel against the Status quo?

As you just read, the status quo is not good for us, or our financial empowerment. The status quo is a hinderance in building financial independence, keeps Neurodivergent people perpetually stuck in ableist systems where we are forced to mask, and abandon who we truly are. Ultimately, the status quo leaves us burned out, feeling unworthy and feeling inadequate. It makes us feel broken because the expectations are unrealistic. How do we rebel against a system designed to hinder us, and destroy our self-worth?

Seek accommodations at work.

First off, take a few career and personality assessments to learn your strengths and weaknesses. Take self-inventory and find out how Neurodivergence impacts you. How is neurodivergence your superpower? In what situations does Neurodivergence hinder you. This is different for everyone. Once you know this, it will be easier to target jobs that are more suited to your strengths.

Secondly, seek out employers and jobs that are more inclusive, and willing to accommodate you. Determining the type of work environment that is inclusive can also make you more willing to disclose.

Determine what accommodation you need. You might find it helpful to review the types of accommodation you had in school.

The Americans with Disabilities Act entitles you to reasonable accommodations. Don't be ashamed to exercise this right.

Deciding whether to disclose?

My personal rule of thumb is to disclose once I see that the employer has a strong history of inclusivity. If disclosing to request accommodations, it is best to do so as soon as possible after

accepting a new job.

If you get into a job and later find that you need accommodation, that's also acceptable as well. It isn't always apparent immediately what challenges a job might present.

Self-advocacy is so important in our financial and career journey. Requesting work accommodation shows you just how imperative self-advocacy is.

Consider entrepreneurship.

Creating your own job is a powerful option. You can bypass the nonsense of employer discrimination, office politics, toxic social situations, and having to mask your Neurodivergence to make a living. Entrepreneurship gives you the power to create a career that is based on your interests, plays up your strengths and boosts your self-esteem knowing that you created a pathway for yourself.

Entrepreneurship inherently comes with risk. Many times, the reward is worthwhile despite this fact.

Travel the world!

Traveling the world has the potential to ward off career, school, and even burnout from living in your home country as a Neurodivergent person. Travel also gives you confidence, teaches you adaptability, independence and introduces you to new people. When you travel the world, you can potentially save money.

Geographic Arbitrage is one of the benefits of traveling the world. If you live in a country with a strong currency, you can travel to countries with weaker currency and enjoy a higher quality of life while traveling.

Traveling the world also opens you up to business ideas, business ideas and career opportunities.

There is a wealth of programs out there that pay you to travel the world (either through jobs, or volunteering).

Traveling is not some rich affluent kid's frivolous pursuit. Traveling is a wealth builder when done the right way.

There are some things to keep in mind when using travel to build wealth:

Cost of living

Taxes

How your expenses might differ from your expenses at home.

Hidden costs

For example: Moving to another state to accept a higher paying job? Make sure the cost of living makes the salary worthwhile. If you're currently living in Alabama earning $45k per year, a $65k a year position in Seattle is NOT an up-level. Due to the cost of living in Seattle, your standard of living will be LOWER despite earning more money on the paper surface. You may also encounter a different real estate market in your new location as well (eg: Broker's fees and heavier deposits are common in the Northeast, whereas the Southeast typically has lower deposits and brokerage fees are unheard of when renting an apartment).

Even with Geographic Arbitrage that I mentioned earlier, there may still be hidden costs where you choose to relocate to. There might also be compromises that you'd have to make as well in order to save such a large sum (the cost of sending money home to pay existing bills, the cost of having to buy bottled water because the tap water in a location is unsafe, etc...)

Traveling in order to increase financial gain isn't without it's risks, so carefully research all of the options and possibilities before booking and boarding those flights.

An alternate approach to saving

Although working extra hours, getting a side hustle etc....is a viable option to help boost your savings. Consider more passive ways to earn money. Creating digital products has the potential to be lucrative. Another example could be renting out a room on platforms like AirBnB, or Home Away. Renting out your cars on a car sharing platform like Turo (I personally did this and found it lucrative) is another option. I suggest looking for ways to pad your pockets with little effort. There are some inherent risks associated with the examples I gave. They are worth exploring though.

Investing:

Investing comes with its own risk, but the rewards can be amazing. Saving for retirement is of utmost importance because as we can see; the government is unreliable and cannot be trusted to take care of us in old age. With the rising cost of living, compound interest from investing will help you be able to weather the storm in the future. It's never too late, it's never too early. You don't have to have a huge chunk of money to start either. You can start small. Just to name a few options: A Roth IRAs, Stocks, Bonds, mutual funds, 401 K retirement plans etc... Investing is a sticky topic and can be a risky endeavor. I advise speaking with a qualified financial professional to help you decide your best option.

A word (some words) about debt

Racking up credit card debt is common for those who earn low income, or inconsistent income. If you find yourself using your credit cards for necessities, to make ends meet; you may eventually find it hard to keep up with your payments. Eventually you will fall behind on payments and default.

When default happens, the credit card gets closed. The credit card companies will try to sell us on debt management plans, payment plans etc…. to pay on a CLOSED ACCOUNT.

Don't fall for that.

You'll essentially be throwing good money after bad.

Paying off a closed credit card in full doesn't raise your credit score at all.

It can be more cost effective to allow the default to land in collections, then settle it for a fraction of what you owe.

In many cases, you can even DISPUTE the collection and get it deleted from your credit report entirely.

If you find yourself in a situation where you've defaulted on a credit card, the situation isn't hopeless. The banks want to make you believe that so that they can make money off you.

Student Loans:

There are several payments plans offered for Federally backed student loans, that will reduce your student loan monthly payments to ZERO. Income Based, Income Contingent REPAYE plans.

Working for a non-profit, government, or publicly funded entity (eg: a not-for-profit university) can make you eligible for the Public Service Student Loan forgiveness after 10 years.

There is also the option for Total Permanent Disability discharge.

You can achieve this either through a Social Security disability determination, a Physician's certification of your disability or the being a Disabled Veteran as determined by the Veteran's Administration.

Please Note: These forgiveness and management pathways apply to Federal Student Loans only.

If you've taken out private student loans, I suggest contacting your bank/servicer to learn what options you have.

Medical Debt:

Medical bills are negotiable by reaching out to the hospital themselves and seeking financial assistance programs offered by the hospital.

A little-known secret that these hospitals don't tell you: They get all kinds of government funding. They HAVE the resources to help those in need. If you inquired about their hardship programs, you can most likely get the debt written off entirely.

Bankruptcy:

If your debts feel overwhelming, and you are threatened with garnishments, lawsuits, levies etc…. Bankruptcy is a good option. Despite the stigma attached to it, Bankruptcy is often more profitable for your bottom line than trying to keep up with debts you can't repay. It isn't a permanent drop to your credit score, as banks will make you believe. There is no shame in seeking this option either if you find yourself in an untenable situation.

These are some ways to manage debt that improve your ability to be financially empowered, independent and free. It comes down to knowledge, and changing our mindset around how we view debt. The first step to fixing it is to overcome our shame around it.

CHAPTER 5

Relationships and Your Money

Relationship Rules and Your MONEY

Keep your finances and your financial goals private.

I've found that when you reveal your finances and financial goals to others too quickly, you end up sabotaging them.

Let's say you have a goal to travel full time for 1 year. You find side hustles and cut off spending in other categories to make this happen. You have already mapped out a plan as to how much you'll spend traveling, when you'll take off and how much you'll need to have saved to feel comfortable.

The problem comes when you reveal your plans to the wrong people early on. The people you reveal your goals to might discourage you from doing so, might speak negatively about your dreams, and even give you all the reasons you shouldn't. The people you're sharing this with might have good intentions, but they don't always have the vision to see your dreams as possible. People also have a habit of projecting their fears onto you as well.

That negative energy will plant seeds of doubt in your mind and cause you to give up on your plans before you even begin.

There are also people who will actively try to sabotage you. When they know you're saving money, they'll try all manner of ways to get you to spend your money.

The roommate who incurs extra bills and expects you to pay them.

The friend who invites you to expensive outings, tempting you to overspend.

The colleague who sees you dressed in a certain outfit, and decides they are entitled to "forget their wallet", and leave you stuck with the bill because you "look like you have money."

The list could go on...

It's better not to reveal financial goals like these UNTIL they're set and stone, when you're DEEP into them.

By the time it's done, your plans are sealed and set; any attempts to sabotage you won't work. You'll be less likely to give up on your plan or goal because either you're too deep into it or you've already accomplished it.

Finding people you can trust to discuss money with.

Everyone needs one person in their life, with whom they can discuss money, financial struggles, financial goals and aspirations with who will be supportive and nonjudgmental. A few qualities this person in your life should possess:

1. They don't belittle you. They don't tell you your dreams are foolish, your goals are shallow, or convince you that your financial dreams are too big for you to accomplish,
2. They don't shame you or make you feel inadequate for your financial struggles.
3. They're willing to learn with you on your financial journey.
4. They support your dreams and root for you.
5. They never make you feel bad for wanting more for yourself.
6. They hold you accountable for reaching your goals and striving to do better for yourself financially.
7. If you ever need it; they offer financial assistance without making you feel bad for needing it.

These are some of the qualities you need to look for when knowing who to trust to talk about money with.

Red Flags to avoid:

When a friend, relative, or partner is generous with everyone else except you. They are willing and able to invest in everyone else; but when it's you, they're stingy and full of excuses.

Someone who uses money to control you. They give you a place to live, an "allowance", or even something as small as a ride somewhere; they give you these things and feel entitled to belittle you. In their mind, they "bought" you and feel entitled to treat you however they wish. AVOID these people like a pandemic. Whatever it is they're giving you isn't worth the long-term trauma these relationships inflict.

A pocket-watcher. This is the person who monitors you, watches you from afar with how you dress, where you go, what you buy; and makes snap judgments on how much they think you spend. They make snap judgements like this to determine if/how they can take advantage of you. An example: a friend of yours constantly asks for favors, or to borrow money. They've observed how you dress, and noticed you treated yourself to a nice purse. They decided you owning that purse entitles them to borrow money from you or leave you with the bill at a restaurant outing. Pocket-watchers are ridiculously toxic.

One of the biggest influences on our money: relationships. Who we allow into our lives, entertain, and spend the most time with can make or break our bottom line. Keep these things in mind when evaluating your circle.

CHAPTER 6

No Confidence No Money

Confidence is an unshakeable belief in yourself, your qualities, and your abilities. Confidence withstands obstacles, naysayers, and trumps self-doubt.

How does this play into our money?

Confidence helps us set healthy boundaries with money, our spending, and how we earn our money.

Self-confidence and self -worth helps you:

Stand firm in your boundaries on what type of work you will do, what pay range you are willing to work for, and what work conditions you are willing to endure.

Know your worth, so that you don't settle for the first opportunity that looks good.

Protecting your peace, energy, and mental health so that you may optimize your earning potential.

The ability to delay gratification for a more substantial financial goal.

Abandon the need to impress others by overspending to keep up with peers.

Go against what society says, and pursue an unconventional career path, and living situation that serves your best interests.

Be willing to say no to a job or opportunity that violates your values, even if the money is great.

Be unafraid to negotiate better terms whether that is working conditions, or large purchases.

Lack of confidence, on the contrary, shows up as lack of belief that we deserve better thus settling for less.

Lack of confidence causes us to:

Stay in places where we are undervalued, overworked, and underpaid.

Not speak up for what we believe we deserve, or when our boundaries aren't being respected.

Being afraid to apply for that job, that speaking engagement, or write that book because we feel we aren't good enough to be in such spaces.

Allowing people to take advance of your generosity out of fear that you won't ever find true friendships.

Believe that you must BUY genuine love and connection.

Overpay for a certain style of clothes to fit in with your peers.

Stay in degrading living situations despite having the resources to move, out of fear that you'll either fail when out on your own, or out of fear that this is the best you can do.

Accept jobs and opportunities that don't value us due to fear of rejection from the opportunities we really want.

Don't misunderstand me here; confidence is NOT the same as being arrogant and thinking of yourself as superior to others.

Confidence lacks the comparison factor; you aren't comparing your worth to other people. Confidence is all about YOU. It's about measuring your progress against your OWN potential, knowing your limits, and celebrating your wins.

In short, lack of confidence keeps you broke and stuck in costly cycles. How do we fix that problem?

There is no shortcut to developing confidence. There isn't one single answer that works for everyone.

From my own life experience, I can share a few things that have helped me gain confidence in myself and my worth:

I am a risk taker. Perhaps growing up without stability and having little to no career options right after college helped me develop this trait. I'm naturally risk aversive, and LIFE had to teach me to be okay taking risks. I was thrust into situations where I had no other choice BUT to take a bet on myself.

I took a bet on myself when I was under pressure to figure out a way to pay for my car expenses after graduation, so I took a chance and rented them out on an online platform called Turo (Relay Rides at the time). I was uncertain. I didn't even know if I could trust the platform. I went in and did it anyway, and discovered an income stream that allowed me to be able to engage in my special interest: travel.

Secondly, I stay to myself and in my own lane. Once again, I've got Autism to thank for that. Socializing less and enjoying my own company allows me to remain confident. Less socializing means you are less influenced by other people's opinions and perceptions of you. You get to know yourself and become sure of who you are. Your identity isn't tied to a clique or a person. Don't get me wrong. Isolation isn't healthy either. I'd say choose a small group of people you can trust to be in your circle, keep them near and dear. However, don't inundate yourself trying to socialize with everyone all of the time. Don't be ashamed to indulge in your alone time.

Third, I've spent my life being drilled that something is always wrong with me as an Autistic person. I easily fell into the trap of not believing in my abilities, and thinking everyone else is better than me. I turned this around by studying Autism advocacy. I connected with like-minded, fellow Autistic people. I've spent time learning about how Autism has been advantageous to me. I've spent my undergraduate years invested in learning some Autistic pride. This was another thing that boosted my confidence.

As an Autistic person, I am gifted with extreme focus, an analytical mind, being inquisitive and being precise. These traits make me amazing to work with (either as an employee or in business). I have traits that are marketable, therefore I know my worth and will not settle for a work situation that treats me as less than.

Fourthly, I hang around positive friends, family and consume positive content that lifts me up, affirms me and always reminds me of my greatness. I don't hang around fake friends who seek to "humble" me (friendship red flag btw). If they don't boost my confidence, they can't be in my world. Simple as that.

Lastly, I practice guilt free self-care. I dress in clothes that make me feel my best. I take long baths and drink my favorite green tea. I cook from scratch whatever I feel like eating. I sleep well, take breaks as needed and get exercise. I travel, read, and enrich myself intellectually.

I say my affirmations. I keep my affirmations posted on social media and on my wall. This is known as reminding yourself of who you ARE!

These are just a few of my tips to build confidence, to eventually make yourself the money you deserve: Self-care, intentional socializing, risk taking, enjoying your alone time and self-advocacy!

Take note: lack of self-confidence will keep you BROKE, overworked, underpaid, and underappreciated.

Lack of confidence will make you vulnerable to people and opportunities that are financially predatory.

Confidence in the long run saves and makes you money.

CHAPTER 7

How it all began: Autism and my relationship with money.

How it began

As an Autistic person, my relationship with money has always been complex.

Money was a constant struggle in my childhood. We struggled to keep stable housing and affording necessities. Money was always tight, and I witnessed my parents stressed about money constantly. The persistent instability continued well into my adulthood when I went off to college; constantly worrying about money, how to pay for college, and how to make ends meet.

Finding and keeping employment was difficult in my college years, due to me having Autism and not understanding my own limitations, how to advocate for myself and how to navigate the social aspects of the workplace.

As a literal thinker, I take everyone at face value. I naturally assume that everyone is straightforward because I am. I've come across supervisors on campus who promised me that if I ever need a job, get in touch with them. When I took them up on the offer, I was either brushed off or given a load of excuses as to why they couldn't hire me. Shortly after, I witnessed those same supervisors hire another candidate. It was a hard lesson in knowing my worth and never begging anyone for a job. I digress. I can write an entire book on this very point.

The bottom line is: Unstable income created a scarcity mindset for me. As soon as I'd get money; I'd hoard it even to my own detriment. Holding on to money rather than paying for necessities, out fear of not knowing when I'd earn my next paycheck.

Unstable income, due to constantly being discriminated against for jobs made me angry and has given me a negative attitude toward paying bills.

Why should I pay rent after I was unjustly let go from a job? Why should I pay high prices for gas, groceries, etc....when I can't even get a fair chance at securing the jobs I deserve?

I went to school, got advanced degrees, and all I'm offered is a job cleaning?? Hell NO I'm not paying ANY bills.

I'll hoard the money for myself, or I'll spend the money on something that brings me joy.

My behavior with money was my way of saying: F-K the system. Since I live this life being passed over for gainful employment that I deserve and am more than qualified for, being dismissed from a job because of b.s. social cues; then F-K it! Why should I spend money "adulting"?

After I graduated from college; and went through endless rejections for job opportunities; I rented my cars out on a platform called Turo; decided to lead the Nomad life and spend my money on Travel: a lifelong passion and dream of mine.

I decided to pursue my dreams as an act of rebellion against a messed up, unfair system.

The intricacies Autism and money management

As an Autistic person, I am a very literal, black-white thinker. This translates into how I manage money:

Not realizing I could have settled medical bills for LESS and stressed myself out trying to pay them off in full.

Taking debt collector's words at face value, not realizing how much negotiating power I have over payment terms.

Not understanding how to prioritize bills: used limited funds to pay off credit card, instead of paying for necessary car repairs, only to end up BACK in debt. I was laser focused on paying off the credit card to the detriment of everything else I needed. I wanted the debt gone by any means necessary.

Executive function struggles, as an Autistic person showed up as:

Getting overwhelmed by multiple bills due at different times of the month; to the point where I'd lose track and forget what to pay and when to pay them.

A few ways I've remedied this:

Moving due dates closer to each other.

Paying bills ahead of time.

Limiting the number of bills I have in the first place. The less bills I have, the easier they are to keep track of and manage. This has by far been my favorite, easiest remedy to that.

A mixture of negative self-image and a literal, black, white thinking mind shows up as:

In the event I couldn't pay a single bill because of an unexpected event; I'd get so angry and rigid about it that I just wouldn't pay ANY bills. It was all or nothing for me.

I'm still on this journey of learning self-love as an Autistic adult and learning how Autism impacts me in various areas of life. The way Autism shows up for me is consistent in all areas of my life. The literalness, need for order, and rigidness is prevalent in my relationship with money.

The move that changed everything for me

After years of struggling to find work in my field, I was offered an opportunity to start a new career path out of state.

At the time, I was working a dead-end job that wasn't Autistic friendly, the sensory environment was hell and it underpaid me. I hated it.

I applied for the new position. It took months to finally get an interview. I aced the interview. I was offered the position.

I was excited and SICK of my current situation, so I jumped on it. While I've done some research on the cost of living in the area, I wasn't thorough enough.

I saw this job opportunity as a chance to prove myself, as a chance to build wealth and finally have self-esteem for myself. My circumstances at the time reinforced the negative self-worth that I had.

I didn't care what it cost me emotionally and mentally.

All I knew was that I wanted to finally experience the self-esteem (and money) that came with getting a job in my field and went for it.

Packed my belongings in my car, drove 18 hours up the coast. I rented a room from a total stranger. Started training for my new job, and eventually made it official.

Things became chaotic shortly after. The housemate I was renting from started relentlessly nitpicking about my mannerisms, my social skills, and just the way I did things (eg; staying to myself a lot). I suspect he picked up on the fact that I have Autism, even before I disclosed it.

Disclosing, I naively thought was for the best, turned out to open the floodgates of abuse. I started to become the butt of jokes, and the last to catch on. Not a day went by where he wasn't finding some reason to complain about me, my mannerisms and make it about my Autism.

He became very controlling, and kept emphasizing that I didn't deserve my position, that I should quit because "Autistic people can't do that job".

I came into this situation already feeling bad about myself because of people who had the same mindset as my housemate about Autistic people.

It didn't end there. My supervisor at my new job, as soon as she learned about me having Autism, tried to talk me into quitting. Although I have no proof, I couldn't ignore the shift in her attitude toward me when she learned.

Being the rebel that I am, I refused to give in. I was determined to stay at that job. When I encounter resistance, it makes me want to stick to it even MORE.

Because of my refusal to quit, she went the extreme spreading vicious lies on me to get me fired. Luckily there was a union backing me, and they protected me. I successfully defended my case and kept my job.

Back to the living situation, my housemate became even more abusive. The situation became so untenable that I ended up inadvertently giving them all their way: I resigned from that job and left that housing situation altogether.

The bullying, targeting and constant abuse at work AND at home became too much to bear.

On top of that, I was living with housemates because the cost of living in the area was too expensive to afford living alone (which is how I best thrive). The pay for the job wasn't enough to afford living alone WHILE saving, investing, and living comfortably. To afford living on my own; I'd have to sacrifice everything that was important to me and live paycheck to paycheck.

That was not acceptable to me.

Moving to another state, taking a professional job; only to struggle makings ends meet and STILL be treated as less than for having Autism taught me several hard lesson:

Getting educated, doing all the "right" things, and obtaining a Professional, "good" state job doesn't guarantee financial stability. It hurt more than ever when I came to terms with the fact that I did all the "right" things and STILL couldn't afford a comfortable life.

Being educated, and working a prestigious job didn't shield me from the bullying that comes with being Autistic. I continued to be overlooked, talked down to, the butt of jokes and taken advantage of emotionally. I had the goal of improving my self-esteem when I moved up there to take that position. That experience did NOTHING for my self-esteem. It reinforced the negative self-image I had.

In short: money, prestige and a career don't always equal self-worth.

Lastly, a high salary in a high cost of living area is meaningless. I realized I was actually better off earning LESS money in a low to moderate cost of living area. This is why it's so imperative to thoroughly investigate the cost of living when receiving a job offer. By thorough investigation, I mean go deeper than an internet search. Take it a step further and talk to people who are from the area, make phone calls to landlords about what the charge for move-in costs, etc..

The lessons I've learned from that experience forever changed my view of jobs, careers, and money. It taught me my values, what is most important to me, and it's redefined what I choose to prioritize not only in my finances but life in general.

I was able to come back from this experience, something that was supposed to destroy my Autistic pride, and have a stronger sense of Autistic pride.

Experiences like this make me passionate about teaching my fellow neurodivergent people a new mindset and new ways to make money than the status quo that's been thrown our way from the time we were conceived.

It's why I do what I do.

ABOUT SHALESE

Shalese Heard is an online influencer who teaches Autistic adults how to travel the world, gain self-confidence, build financial freedom and self-advocacy. Shalese is an author, YouTuber, and speaker. She obtained Master's degrees in both Business Administration and Environmental Public Health.

Shalese's career is a bit unconventional where she's created her own career. She's spent most of her career self-employed with various entrepreneurial ventures. She started her own car rental business renting out her cars on a car sharing platform. What started out as a side hustle ended up as a full-time living that allowed her the freedom to travel the world. Eventually she has turned her social media endeavors (YouTube, writing, consulting, speaking) into viable income streams.

Throughout her career journey, she struggled with finding her place professionally as an Autistic person. She also realized the importance of financial freedom as an Autistic person, that being financially free is imperative for our self-esteem, mental and physical health.

Her own experiences made her passionate about showing other Autistic people ways to create financial freedom for themselves. It all began with her drive and tenacity to find income streams to fund her special interest: world travel. In her spare time, she enjoys fashion, jumping waves at the beach, going to the spa and cooking new recipes.

Full Disclaimer:

The information in this book is NOT a substitute for professional financial advice, or legal advice. Although the tips I've shared in here work for myself and many others, they don't apply to everyone's unique situation. Therefore, discretion is advised.

Made in United States
Orlando, FL
16 June 2024

47952424R00022